NORTH VALLEY MIDDLE SCHOOL

```
                                        7.95
   914.3
   HIL
       Hills, C. A. R.
          The Rhine
```

```
                                        7.95
   914.3
   HIL
       Hills, C. A. R.
          The Rhine
```

DATE DUE	BORROWER'S NAME
MAY 1 1995	Sara Ramaker 7-E

NORTH VALLEY MIDDLE SCHOOL

The Rhine

The Rhine begins high up in the Swiss Alps as two foaming streams, fed by hundreds of icy trickles. It descends rapidly into a land of sheltered pastures, then leaves Switzerland for its long journey to the North Sea through extremes of great natural beauty and grim industrial development.

In this book we follow the Rhine from source to delta, examining its cities, people, industry, and place in history and legend. We look too at the results of human intervention: control of the river's flow, and the great problems of pollution.

Frontispiece *Many areas of the Rhine are famous for their wines. Here, the vineyards at Rudesheim grow down to the river's edge.*

Rivers of the World

NORTH VALLEY MIDDLE SCHOOL

The Rhine

C A R Hills

Wayland/Silver Burdett

Rivers of the World

The Amazon
The Danube
The Ganges
The Mississippi
The Nile
The Rhine

Copyright © 1979 Wayland Publishers Limited.
First published in 1979 by
Wayland Publishers Limited
49 Lansdowne Place, Hove
Sussex BN3 1HF, England
ISBN 0 85340 455 0

Published in the United States by
Silver Burdett Company, Morristown,
New Jersey.
1978 printing.
ISBN 0 382 06202 7

Phototypeset by Trident Graphics Limited, Reigate Surrey
Printed in England by Loxley Brothers Limited.

Contents

The River and the Highway	9
The Alpine Stream	15
Into the Rift Valley	25
Through the Rhine Gorge	35
From Bonn to the Ruhr	45
The Rhine Delta	53
Glossary	62
Facts and Figures	63
Further Reading	64
Index	65

The River and the Highway

The Rhine is not by any means one of the longest rivers in the world, but it is one of the greatest and busiest. It is only 1,320 km (820 miles) in length; it drains water from an area about the same size as England, Scotland and Wales together – which is not impressive by world standards. Yet it washes the borders or heartlands of no less than six European states – Switzerland, Liechtenstein, Austria, West Germany, France and Holland – and flows through tremendously varied and busy landscapes.

It begins as a turbulent Alpine stream with great floods in spring when the ice melts. Later it receives half a dozen important tributary rivers and develops into a broad, powerful river with an exceptionally steady and even flow. It flows northwards through regions of varied upland and lowland and then pours forth into the North Sea in a large and complicated delta.

The chief importance of the Rhine is that it has always been a great line of human movement, settlement and communications. The remains of very early man have been found near Düsseldorf. As early as Roman times, two thousand years ago, river traffic was so great that the Romans set up an organized system of customs and tolls. In modern times more than 200 million tonnes of cargo pass up and down the river every year. Through canal links being built with other great rivers, such as the Rhône and Danube, the Rhine will shortly be at the very centre of a waterway system spanning the whole of Europe. Many other rail and road routes either cross or run alongside it.

Along the banks of the river lie a string of great cities containing tens of millions of people.

Left *The Rhine at the beginning of its long journey from the Alps to the North Sea*

Above *A Roman theatre at Augst, near Basel*

Right *A scene by the Rhine at Basel*

The suburbs of these cities are now tending to run into each other. It seems as if there is a single giant city developing along the Rhine – what geographers call a megalopolis. There are some beautiful unspoilt stretches along the river still, but this intense development brings with it a typical modern problem – pollution.

Although the Rhine is an international river, for more than half its course it flows through West Germany. To the Germans the Rhine is in many ways a sort of national symbol; much of their folklore and history is connected with it and many famous Germans were born along its banks. But, tragically, ever since it formed the borders of the Roman Empire, two thousand years ago, the Rhine has been a battle-ground. The Rhine has been the scene of fighting for many different peoples: the Celts, Huns, Russians, Swedes, French, Danes and Hungarians – as well as the Germans – have all ruled over it. In our own century some of the last and most desperate battles of the Second World War were fought around here. As we travel along the Rhine we shall learn something of its troubled but exciting history.

In the much vaster geological time-scale, the Rhine is a young river. The mountains where it begins, the Alps, were pushed up in great folds

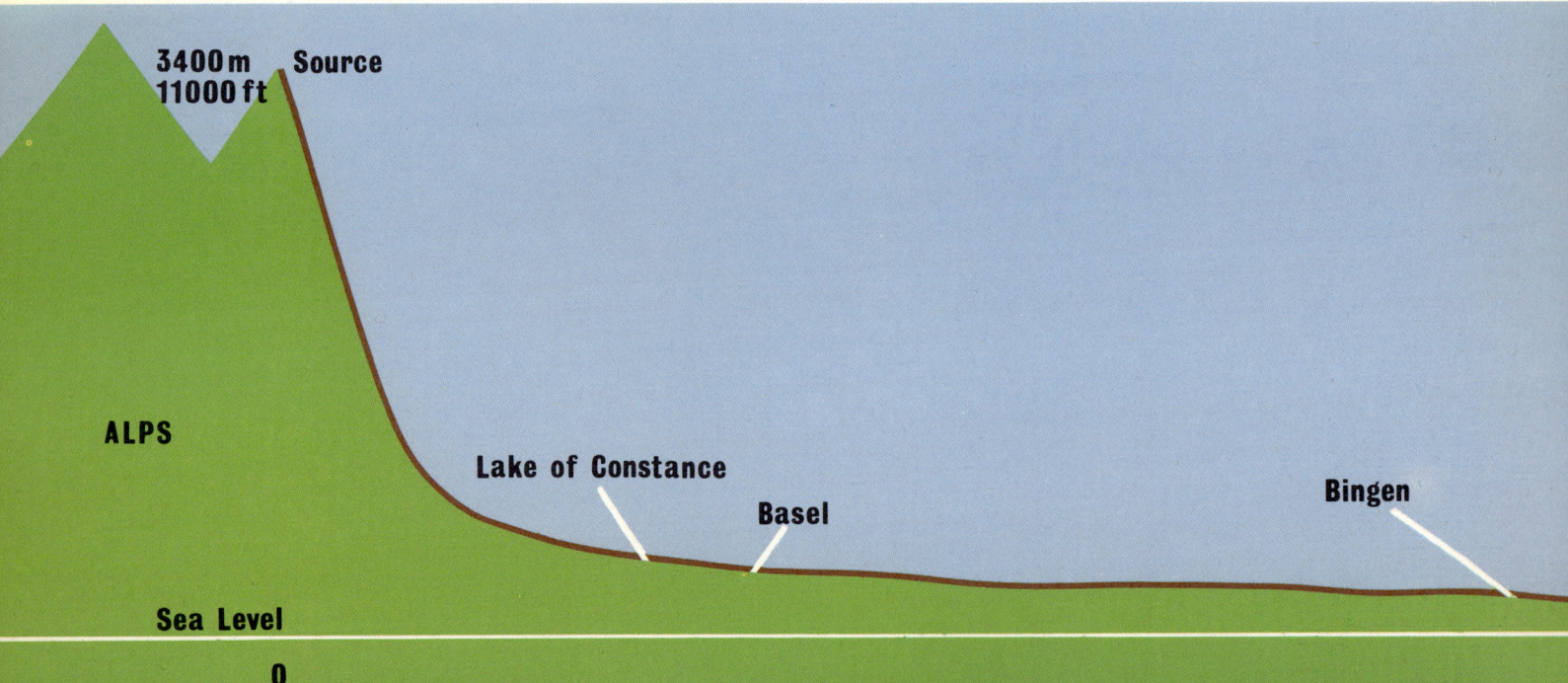

A cross-section diagram, showing the course of the Rhine from the Alps to the North Sea.

Bonn   Köln

RHINE

North Sea

1320 kms | 820 miles

Above *Because of pollution, otters like these are now only found near the source area of the Rhine*

from sea deposits in a period of earth disturbances about 30 million years ago. As the Rhine travels northwards it flows through even older mountains, the Central European Highlands. These were originally formed in the same way as the Alps, but much longer ago. They have since been worn down, submerged under the sea and split up under the pressure of the building of the Alps to the south. Since the time the Alps were formed, the Rhine has carried a great deal of rocky, muddy material down with it to form its lower course and delta.

During the Ice Ages, when Britain was joined to the European continent, the Rhine flowed as far north as what is now Norway and Sweden. When the ice melted, the sea level rose and the river's present course was created.

We are going to travel down the river from source to mouth, noting interesting features on our way. We shall start in the high, icy Alps and then follow the Rhine on its busy and varied course.

Right *A bridge over the Hinter Rhine*

The Alpine Stream

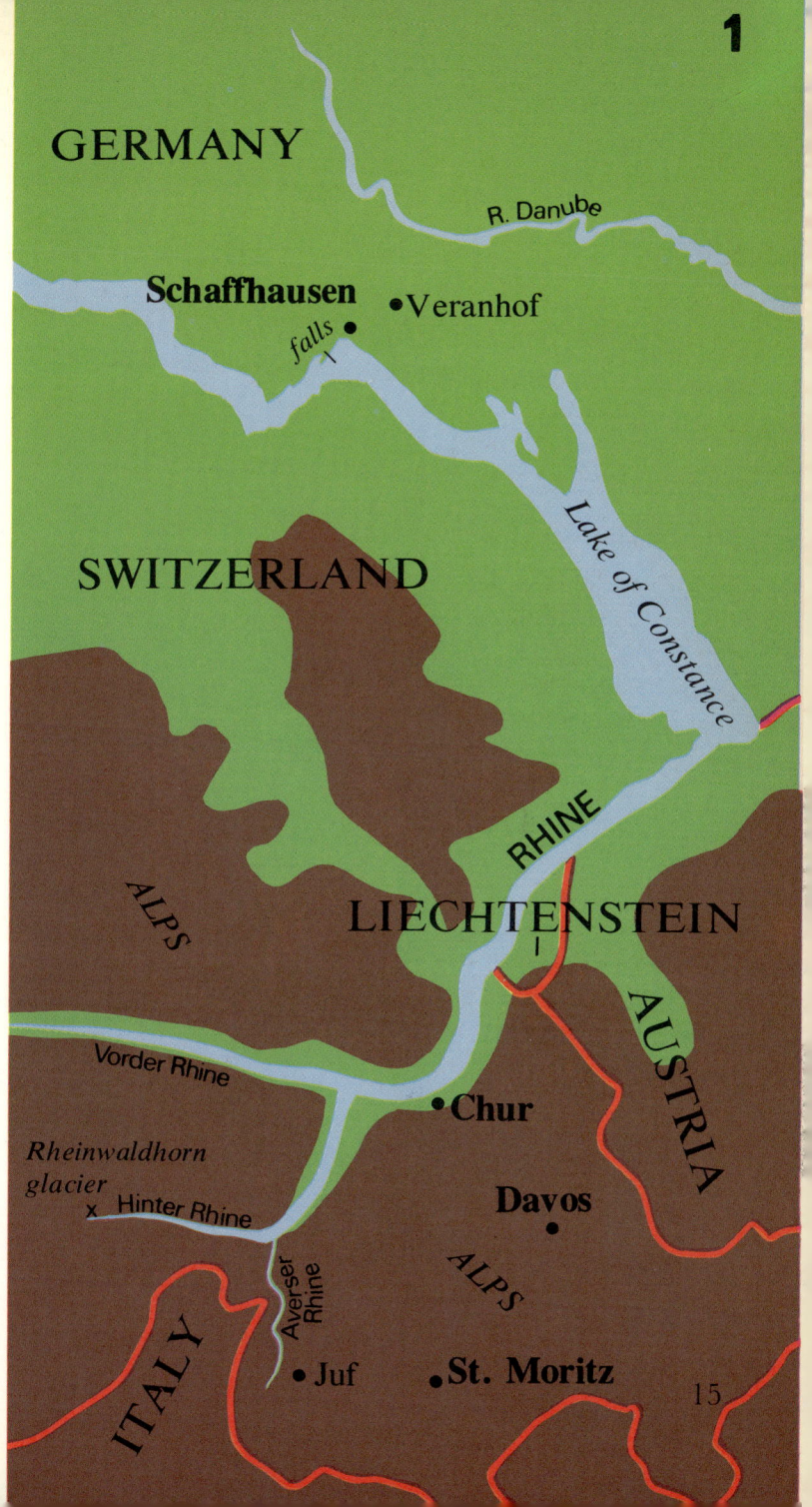

It is often very difficult to tell exactly where a river starts, for many channels may come together to form a greater stream. Where the Rhine is concerned, though, tradition says that the most powerful and highest source really is *the* source. This is the Rheinwaldhorn Glacier, a vast shell of ice found about 3,400 m (11,000 ft) up in the Swiss canton (district) of the Grisons. Here there is eternal snow. This great icefall coats a snowy peak; from under a cave in the ice a brook emerges, in little rivulets swollen with glacial mud. It flows steeply down towards the valley and passes through a high gorge which the local farmers call "Hell". This is the Rhine at the start of its long journey.

This main headstream of the Rhine is called the Hinter Rhine. It flows at first through a tremendously rugged and isolated part of the Swiss Alps. The vigorous young river is a powerful cutting agent for it falls steeply: 1½ km (1 mile) in the first 72 km (45 miles) of its journey.

In its steep valley, as in other Alpine valleys, the people follow a distinct way of life which has developed over centuries. It is only now becoming a little more modern. This way of life

Left *A typical Alpine landscape by the Hinter Rhine*

Above *Snowy scene near the Rheinwaldhorn glacier*

involves herding animals and a little growing of crops in sunny valley bottoms. Sometimes the people and their animals move up the mountainside in spring, past pine trees to the high summer pastures just below the level of the snow. On one other nearby source of the Rhine, the Averser Rhine, is found Juf, the highest inhabited village of the Alps, at about 2,000 m (7,000 ft). It can be a beautiful place in summer with Alpine flowers spread out over the valley, but in winter it is cold and bleak indeed. Many of the houses are deserted; those that are lived in burn peat continuously to keep the inhabitants warm!

After running through its valley a little way, the Rhine rushes through another gorge and through pine woods, to come out as a torrent into the little valley of Schams. Nearby are famous ski resorts such as Davos and St. Moritz, but this is an isolated valley. Here the people speak an interesting language called Romansch, which is spoken fairly widely in the canton of the Grisons. Most people in Switzerland speak either German or French, but the people of the Grisons were cut off for centuries and their language is a survival of ancient Latin. Although it is only spoken by a small number of Swiss, it has been recognized as an official language.

At the end of this valley we come to one of the most spectacular sights of our journey – the deep and narrow gorge that the ancient Romans called the "Via Mala" or Evil Way. The river

Right *The Evil Way gorge. Many Roman soldiers fell to their deaths from these fearsome cliffs*

swirls downwards between huge, black-slate cliffs, almost 500 m (1,600 ft) high and, at one point, only 3 m (10 ft) apart. This was often a fateful width for the Romans, because there is no easy way across the Alps at this point. Many unfortunate Roman soldiers lost their footing edging their way along these fearsome cliffs.

The Rhine now passes into a more open valley and flows through the pretty medieval walled town of Chur, a market centre for this region. At

Below   *The pretty little Swiss town of Chur*

Above *The town of St. Gallen, between Liechtenstein and the Lake of Constance*

Reichenau it collides at right-angles with the other main source of the Rhine – the Vorder Rhine. This river began life from a great lake beneath a crag and has reached here fed by glacier streams and mountain waterfalls. The green torrent now flows into a lower and less forbidding landscape – the canton of Appenzell, where the snow peaks are a little further away. Nearby are lakes, pastures, forests and flowers.

For a time now the Rhine is a frontier with Austria and, before that, with the tiny state of Liechtenstein, with Switzerland on the western

Right *The monument marking the junction of Switzerland, France and Germany, at Basel*

side. Europe has a number of small states like Liechtenstein. Often they are remnants of medieval principalities, which have never been tidied up into the modern political map. When Germany became a united country in 1871, Liechtenstein was somehow forgotten. The people of this little country are intensely proud of the independence of their 160 square km (61 square miles) of land. They love the Rhine too, although it has occasionally been a dangerous enemy, for there are sometimes great floods in its tempestuous upper region. In 1927 a great flood burst the river banks and covered half of the entire country! As technology improves, however, very great control has been gained over the river in this area.

The political geography of this region is very complex. As well as dividing Switzerland from Liechtenstein and Austria, as the Rhine approaches the Lake of Constance there is a

Below *A small, peaceful corner of the Lake of Constance*

patchwork frontier with Germany (France is also quite nearby). Beyond the lake, the little village of Veranhof, with three families and a few farm plots was, until recently, German territory surrounded entirely by Switzerland!

The Lake of Constance itself (called the Boden See in German) is a tremendously spectacular sight, more than three times bigger than the country of Liechtenstein. In summer it is crowded with pleasure boats of all kinds. This lake has also been helpful in the control of floods because it can be used as a vast water expansion tank -- for days at a time the lake will release at its northern end only a tenth of the water it receives from the Alpine course.

Now the river, swollen by ever-increasing waters, falls over many rapids and over its great waterfall at Schaffhausen. This is as far as boats can reach from the sea. The first type of craft we see will probably be pleasure boats, but the character of the Rhine is quickly changing. We are soon leaving Switzerland and the lonely beauty of the Alpine course, for the river is becoming a great commercial artery flowing through the prosperous towns and cities of central Europe. As we approach Basel we start on this new section of our journey.

Left *The main set of falls on the Rhine, at Schaffhausen*

Into the Rift Valley

As we leave Switzerland behind we come to a very different section of the river: the rift valley. For a great distance between the towns of Basel and Bingen, the full-grown and powerful river flows through a plain generally about 30 km (20 miles) wide, with hills all along each side, some of which are in Germany and some in France. In ancient geological times a hill-mass covered this whole area, but in the period of earth disturbance when the Alps were built, lines of weakness running parallel in the rocks developed. These lines of weakness are called faults. A belt of country was let down between these lines, where the river now flows. Wherever this type of feature is found in the world it is called a rift valley. Geologists in modern times first came to understand rift valleys by studying this region. Some of them even believe that these lines of weakness continue under the Alps so that the rift here may be connected in some way to the larger rifts of the Jordan Valley and East Africa.

We enter the rift valley suddenly through a gap in the mountains. Here, on the river in Switzerland near where it meets both France and Germany, a great international city has grown

Left *An aerial view of Basel*

Right *Basel harbour. This is as far as larger boats can reach from the North Sea*

up – Basel (sometimes known by its French title of Basle). Many international routes meet here and since 1901 the Rhine has been improved to make it navigable for shipping. So Basel, far away from the sea, is a port receiving many of the raw materials used in the highly-skilled Swiss industries. It also has many industries of its own.

But this great development brings with it a typical modern problem – pollution. The Rhine is still a very dirty river indeed, in spite of the efforts that are now being made on an international scale to clean it up. The outstanding success the English have had in cleaning the Thames gives hope for the Rhine. The trouble really became serious at the time of the Industrial Revolution two hundred years ago. At one time there were so many salmon in the Rhine that workers at Basel were given this fish to eat. Salmon, however, need clean water if they are to pass upstream from the sea. Once the lower river became polluted, no more salmon were found in the whole length of the Rhine. However, it seems the situation is improving! On August 4th, 1978 it was reported that two salmon had been caught in the Rhine Gorge area.

Beyond Basel we travel into the rift valley. The plain is wide, but hills, often made of hard granite, can be seen on the horizon. The river

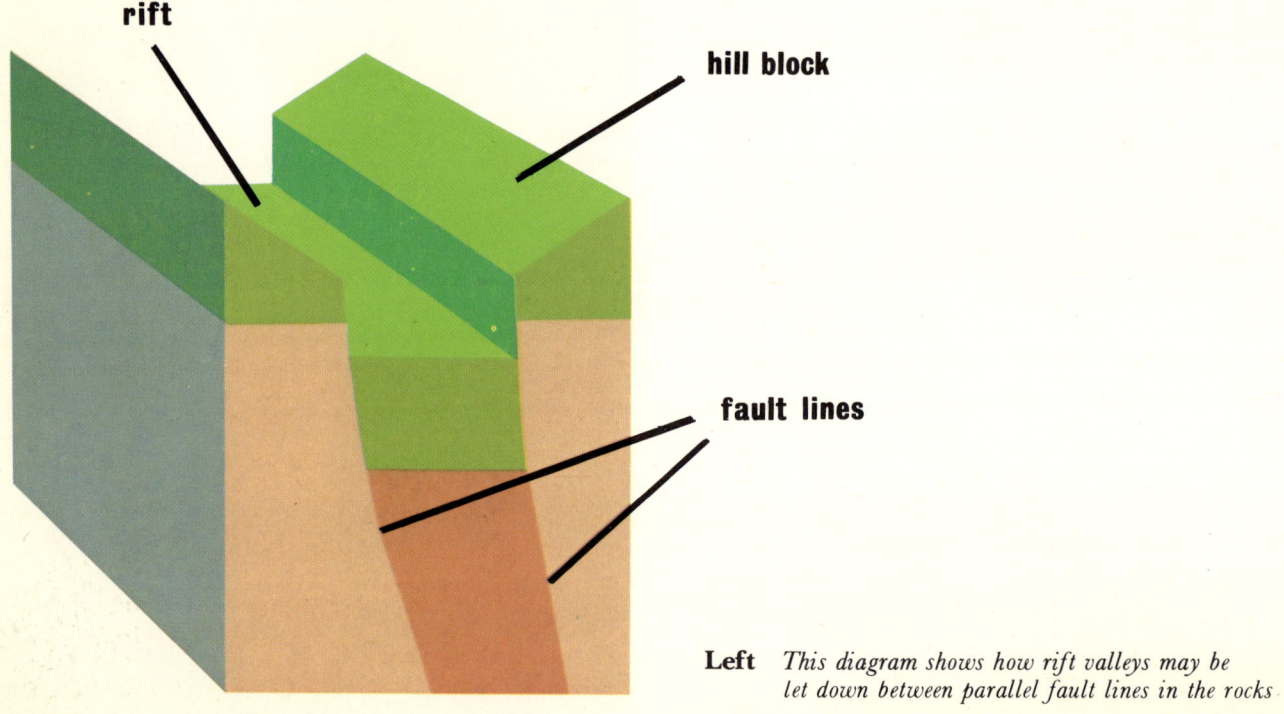

Left *This diagram shows how rift valleys may be let down between parallel fault lines in the rocks*

26

Below *The edge of the Black Forest*

here marks the boundary between France and Germany; to one side is the German Black Forest, to the other the French Vosges. The hilltops are windy and covered with coarse grass. Below the grass is a belt of dark forest and then, on the more cheerful lower slopes, there are orchards, vineyards, gardens and many medieval villages. The valley floor is uneven; it has a warm climate and many colourful crops (including wheat, tobacco, fruit and vines) are grown in the fields between the busy towns and cities.

Above *A German wine-grower tending a vine*

On the frontier, the river often flows on sandy patches amid trees and these areas still seem rather rural. Along the banks there are terraces — patches of higher ground which mark the former course of the river before it cut down deeply. Many farming settlements are found on these terraces. A few volcanic hills rise steeply from the plain, making the landscape very dramatic.

In its natural state, the river flowed across the plain in various channels and loops or meanders, but in the nineteenth century, when traffic became heavier, the river course was straightened out. However, there are still islands in the river, behind which boats often seem to disappear! In France a canal has been cut between Basel and Strasbourg which has taken much of the river traffic from the Rhine.

Above *The old port of Strasbourg with the cathedral in the background*

30 **Above** *Wealthy Europeans enjoying themselves at Baden-Baden in the early nineteenth century*

On the German side of the river, the towns – such as the pleasant university town of Freiburg – tend to be a little away from the river. On the French side, we soon come to an important city – Strasbourg, the beautiful and historic capital of the French province of Alsace. Strasbourg is an important river port with a very famous ancient cathedral. This great building stands out amid the orange-coloured roofs where storks often come to nest. The town's history mirrors the troubled story of this region; from its beginning as a Celtic frontier settlement, it has been attacked many times. During the last century it has belonged at different periods to both France and Germany. Now, happily, European conflict has given way to co-operation and harmony, so Strasbourg is firmly established as a very French city. One of its most famous products is goose liver pâté (pâté de foie gras). The method of making this involves some cruelty to the geese, for they have to be literally stuffed with food to fatten them. The pâté, however, is exceedingly tasty!

On the German side of the river, a little way from the bank, we come to Baden-Baden; this was a famous spa – one of the health resorts that were very popular with wealthy Europeans during the nineteenth century. Here people bathed in waters which were said to cure illness.

Near Karlsruhe, an important industrial town, the Rhine flows into exclusively German territory. About 60 km (40 miles) to the north, where the Rhine meets its first great tributary the River

Above *A street and cafe in Freiburg*

Left *Mannheim, a typical modern German city*

Neckar, we come to a whole group of important towns around the port of Mannheim. These great urban conurbations (very large, built-up areas where several towns run together) are now found along the Rhine like a series of giant beads on a string. Industries have grown so much in this area that firms have been forced to seek new waterside sites for factories at such places as Worms and Speyer – once sleepy medieval towns famous for their cathedrals. Workers in the industries live in all the surrounding villages of the conurbation.

Worms is especially famous in German history because it was here, in 1521, that the great religious reformer Martin Luther came to face the Imperial Diet (the ruling body of Germany at that time) who wanted him to give up his new Protestant doctrines. His answer to them at the end of his speech: "Here I stand. I can not do otherwise. Amen." has gone ringing on through history as the first great example of that new independent spirit that the Protestant Reformation brought to European people. Half the people in Germany today are Protestants and half are Roman Catholics. The people who live on the Rhine banks, in spite of Luther, are still mainly Catholics.

North of this great group of towns, the hills on either side of the plain are mainly made of limestone and are lower than those we passed earlier. On their slopes are many vines, for we have entered the great wine-producing area of Germany.

The river bends westwards near the ancient Roman city of Mainz. It is now very powerful and wide. Many of the famous German light white wines are grown in this area, which is called the Rheingau. Once again there is a great conurbation nearby, around the important city of Frankfurt, but near the river itself the country is beautiful and rural still. To the north rise the dark mountains of the Taunus. In the plain there are many poplar trees, vines and small grey houses with white shutters.

But this peaceful landscape is soon to give way to a more dramatic one. Suddenly the river narrows and mountains loom up on either side by the very edges of the river. We are leaving the wide and cheerful plain – for the Rhine Gorge.

Above *Luther, on the right in friar's robes, faces the Imperial Diet at Worms to defend his new Protestant doctrines*

Through the Rhine Gorge

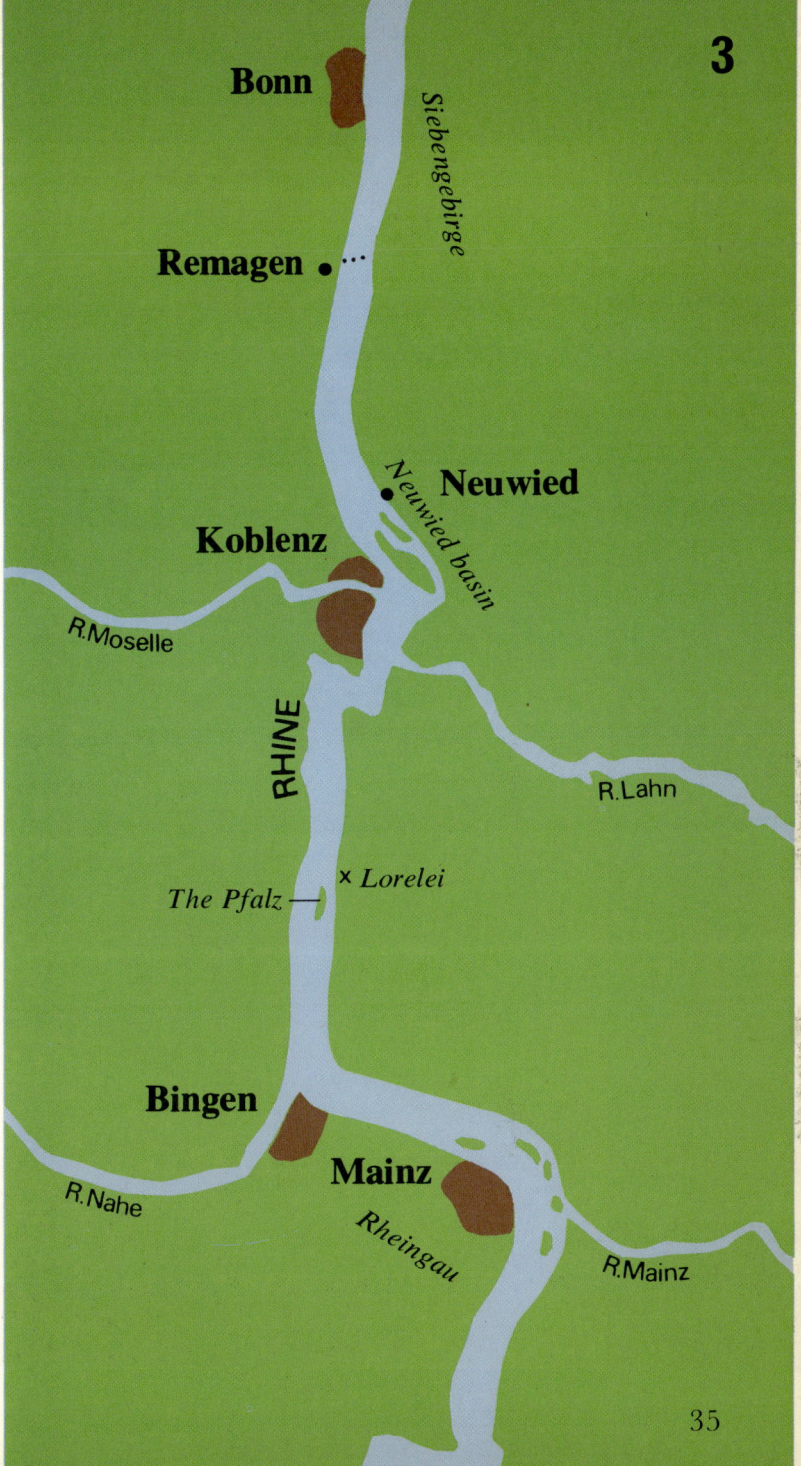

For more than 80 km (50 miles) from Bingen to just above Bonn, the Rhine travels through its steep gorge. The wide plain has given way to a narrow valley that is sometimes less than 180 m (200 yds) across. This valley is surrounded by high mountains and, in places, by sheer cliffs. These mountains were originally formed 200 million years ago, when a great mountain block covered the entire area. This block was later worn down but, when the Alps were built 30 million years ago, it was uplifted and shattered by great earth pressures. It split into hill fragments and the Rhine carved its gorge through a gap in these hills.

The southern section of the gorge, between Bingen and Koblenz, is tremendously spectacular. On the slopes of the mountains are many ruined castles from which vineyards spread steeply down to the river. Sometimes, where the valley opens out a little, there is a fertile plain with a village or walled town, often with beautiful half-tembered houses. On the higher slopes there may be a mysterious forest while the mountain tops themselves, rarely seen from the valley, are barren and windswept. This is the

Left   *Gutenfels Castle, overlooking the Rhine Gorge*

Above *The Mouse Tower, where according to legend, Bishop Hatto of Mainz was devoured by mice*

sort of romantic landscape that the visitor often associates with Germany, and it is a true picture. However, the river is also very busy with pleasure and commercial craft; the road and rail lines on either side of the valley hum with traffic, which sometimes destroys the medieval atmosphere.

Almost immediately we enter the gorge, however, we see a castle on a rock in the middle of the river. This is the famous Mouse Tower which is connected with the story of Bishop Hatto of Mainz. The legend goes that he was always very quick to collect corn from the peasants but, in times of famine, he hid his corn in a barn and refused to let the starving peasants eat. He suffered a terrible punishment for this cruelty: a swarm of mice pursued him to this castle in the river, where they devoured him.

A little later we come to the Pfalz of Kaub, another castle in the middle of the river. In the Middle Ages it was used to spy on passing shipping and collect taxes from it, but now it serves a happier purpose as a shipping museum. Many of the castles on the heights were also the haunts of robber knights in the Middle Ages who preyed on shipping. Dark tales of murder and torture are told connected with these grim fortresses. Because Germany did not become a united country until 1871, there were still customs barriers set up by the local rulers until about that date. In the late nineteenth century, however, the customs barriers were removed.

On terraced slopes we see hundreds of vines

Above *The Pfalz of Kaub castle, on a small island in the middle of the Rhine*

Above *A view of the Rhine Gorge*

and on little plains there are villages and small towns inhabited almost entirely by wine growers. Even the children of the families are expected to help with the work. When the grapes are picked there is usually a great festival called a "harvest home" where the brass band of the village will play. This must be a good reward for all that hard work! Nowadays many of these towns and villages also earn a lot of money from tourism.

Much of this stretch of the river can be dangerous, very shallow or rocky. River pilots are sometimes used; at bends there are often signal stations with coloured flags to warn of passing ships. Many rocks in the river have been

Above *The famous Lorelei Rock, where legend says a beautiful maiden sang to lure sailors to their doom*

blasted with dynamite to make it safer. The most famous of the danger spots is found about halfway between Bingen and Koblenz – the famous cliff called the Lorelei, which juts out 120 m (400 ft) above a river that is here only 45 m (150 ft) wide. There is a legend that a beautiful maiden called the Lorelei sat there and sang a song that lured innocent sailors to their doom on the rocks. Whatever the truth of this, many ships have come to a sticky end at this dangerous point!

A very famous song about the legend was written in the nineteenth century to words by the great German poet, Heine. People in pleasure boats sing this as they pass the rock. It begins:

> "I do not know what it may mean
> that I am so sad . . ."

But, as well as being a German, Heine was also a Jew and, when Hitler and the Nazis came to power in Germany in 1933, they were faced with a problem – they wanted to banish all traces of the Jews from German life, even eventually going so far as to murder them. This song, however, was too well-known to be banned. So they finally hit on a solution – the song could be sung, but the poem was described as being by an "anonymous author". This was the sort of lie the Nazis were reduced to when imposing their perverted vision of German culture on the German people.

Halfway through the gorge the river broadens out into an area of lowland, the Neuwied Basin, where it is joined by the rivers Lahn and Moselle. Here stands the ancient city of Koblenz, founded by the Romans. Many of these Catholic cities of the Rhineland have great festivals connected with the wine-growing. Koblenz has one connected with the Ice Saints who are the patron saints of the wine-growing area. These German carnivals are much more exciting than English ones – processions are planned for many months; during carnival week there are parties and balls, schools close down and people dance and sing in the streets!

North of Koblenz the gorge becomes lower and less spectacular, but there are still many famous sights. Shortly before the gorge ends we see the stumps of a bridge in the stream – this is the bridge at Remagen which played such an important part in the closing stages of the Second World War. During the war the British and Americans had blown up many sites on the Rhine but in 1945 the Germans still struggled to defend the Rhine bridges. Hitler sent orders that the bridge at Remagen was to be blown up to prevent the Americans crossing into the heartland of Germany and ending the war. The bridge was blown up, but too late, for the Americans had crossed. It is said that Hitler summoned the lieutenant who should have

Right *The River Moselle, a tributary of the Rhine*

Left *Rheinstein Castle*

42 **Above** *A view from the Dragon's Rock, towards the Rhine*

blown up the bridge and, in a fit of rage, personally tore the medals off his uniform! Hitler then had the lieutenant and three other officers executed.

Just as we come out of the gorge, there rise up on our right a great group of hills of volcanic origin – the seven hills or Siebengebirge, so called because there are seven main ones, although a number of smaller ones. Many legends are connected with these hills. In the fairy story of Snow White, it was to a castle on one of these hills that the seven dwarfs are said to have taken Snow White for protection from her evil stepmother. The highest of these hills, the Drachenfels or Dragon's Rock, is connected with the great German legends of the Nibelungs, which form the basis of the beautiful operas of "The Ring of the Nibelungs" by Richard Wagner. It was on the Drachenfels that the young hero Siegfried killed the dragon, who was called Fafner, and received the sword Notung. The Drachenfels has become so famous and popular with tourists that it is said to be the most climbed hill in the world. This may be the reason why litter now appears to be a greater problem on the hill than dragons!

As we pass the Siebengebirge we see on the other side of the river the city of Bonn. We are now leaving the highland course for ever. We pass on to a great region of cities and industry – and on to the flat Northern European Plain through which the river flows on its way to the open sea.

Above *Ancient and modern – a castle with traffic lights for boats*

From Bonn to the Ruhr

We are now entering one of the most astonishing areas of our journey – the greatest industrial and urban region of western Europe. Within a 64 km (40 mile) radius of Düsseldorf live more than ten million people. A very great proportion of German industry is found in this region, especially coal and steel. This is a tremendously busy and exciting area but, like any huge industrial region, it has its problems. Many more people live here than in London, but it is different because here there is a ring of cities rather than one big one. This means that some of the problems that affect London or Paris – the difficulty of getting into the centre, for instance – are not so serious here, but there are equally serious problems.

The northern part of the region – the Ruhr – is the most important coalfield in Europe and, owing to dirty industry, pollution has reached very serious levels. In the southern part of the area are several older towns which are still important, but here too problems of overcrowding, pollution and the worsening quality of life are becoming serious. Some of these problems we must look at as we travel through.

Left *A new bridge over the Rhine at Düsseldorf*

Above *The Rhine is a wide, powerful river by the time it reaches Bonn*

The first important town we reach is Bonn, the capital of West Germany. Until thirty years ago Bonn was only a quiet university town. After its defeat in 1945, Germany gradually became divided into two parts. Berlin, the old capital, fell mainly into Eastern Germany, which came under Communist rule. It was difficult to choose a new capital for West Germany. It was said that it was because the Chancellor, Konrad Adenauer (equivalent of an English prime minister or an American president), had a house nearby that little Bonn was finally chosen.

After the horrors of the Nazi period, the West Germans have made a tremendous success of running a democracy. The Rhine runs past the parliament house, or Bundeshaus, which you may visit to see how the German people are ruled. Bonn has grown very rapidly since it became the capital, but it is still a cheerful and attractive place, more like a small town than the capital of a great country.

Already, by the time we reach Bonn, the traffic on the river is becoming very heavy and the water tremendously dirty. If you went for a swim in the river here, you might need to be treated with a stomach pump! Almost all the fish that used to live in the river have died and, although you sometimes see hopeful people by the water with fishing rods, it is not recorded that they ever catch much. Salt pollution, mainly

Below *Parliament buildings at Bonn*

from France, and phosphate pollution connected with detergents are two of the major problems. Now serious efforts are being made to remedy this shocking state of affairs: an international commission has been set up and there is hope for improvement.

It is about 30 km (20 miles) down the river to the next city, Köln (Cologne as it is known in English). We travel through a landscape that is still fairly rural, although development is taking place fast. Köln is an ancient city founded by the Romans. At its centre is a great medieval cathedral with two spires. During the last war the city suffered terrible destruction from bombing; all the bridges over the Rhine were blown up and most of the buildings flattened. But, although the cathedral was hit a number of times, most of it was left standing. Now it remains in the totally rebuilt city centre, right next to the great new railway station and surrounded by futuristic buildings – a link with the past.

There are many pylons and chimneys by the river as we travel towards the next city, Düsseldorf, a very busy and elegant place which is the capital of this region of Germany. Just north of Düsseldorf, near where the motorway cuts a swathe through limestone cliffs, in a still, quiet gorge, there is the place where remains of Neanderthal man have been found. This was a short, strongly-built kind of man, a sort of cousin to modern man, who lived 100,000 years ago. By this date man had spread from his original home

Left *Köln's famous cathedral and one of its many bridges*

Above *Smoke and chimneys near Düsseldorf*

in Africa near the source of the Nile to northern Europe. Neanderthal man lived in caves and hunted for a living, but he was not anything like as intelligent as modern man.

North of Düsseldorf we approach the great coalfield area of the Ruhr. It is difficult to forget the impression made by this great region of coal and steel. So intense is the activity that a great pall of smoke hangs over the whole area by day while at night the sky burns with red light. By the river we see endless factories, warehouses, blast furnaces, silos, railway sidings and barges at anchor. The Ruhr towns are laid out, in general, from east to west and the Rhine flows through the westernmost big town – Duisburg, the greatest inland port in the world. This is at the junction of the rivers Rhine and Ruhr and the Rhine-Herne Canal. A million people live in this great and dirty city; there are more than 30 km (20 miles) along the rivers which are solely quays for ships. The air is dark with blast furnaces, the ground pitted with coalmines and we hear all about us the never-ending sound of ships' motors.

Rhine river traffic, in fact, is enormous; most of it is found between this area and the sea. In the Middle Ages boats were generally drawn by horses on the banks, but in modern times there are many sophisticated methods. Now barges of up to 2,000 tonnes ply the river; some of these boats are pulled along by diesel tugs, some are propelled from behind by "pushers", but boats and oil tankers with their own engines are now increasingly common. People of different European nationalities work the barges; often a whole family will live on one, in a self-contained little world which may even include closed-circuit television. Supermarkets on boats supply the needs of the barge people.

The Ruhr is a tremendously impressive and ugly industrial region, but it is all contained within one area. A few miles on from Duisburg, at a bend in the river, it seems suddenly to end and the short remaining part of the journey through Germany is through rural country, for now we are approaching the Rhine delta.

Above *Car workers making batteries in the industrial Ruhr area*

Above *The Ruhr, the greatest industrial region of western Europe*

The Rhine Delta

We now pass through Germany into the Netherlands (Holland). The remainder of the course in this country is made up almost entirely of the great delta which the Rhine shares with the rivers Maas and Scheldt. These begin in France as the Meuse and Escaut.

We find a delta at the mouth of a river when the flow suddenly slows down and the rate of sedimentation – the laying down of material by the river – is greater than its removal by the sea. The laying down of so much silty material forces the river to divide into many channels or distributaries. Many of the world's great rivers – such as the Ganges, Mississippi and Nile – end in huge deltas; they are often fertile and heavily-populated areas, but their closeness to the open sea can make them dangerous.

In Holland the land is sinking and often the sea may gain at the expense of the land. Disastrous floods may take place, like the one in January 1953 which claimed thousands of lives. The Dutch people have responded magnificently to the challenge, however. They have reclaimed and saved much land from the sea, never forgetting the national motto which is engraved into the dyke that protects the Zuider Zee, the great

Left *A picture taken from space of the combined deltas of the Rhine and the Meuse (bottom right of the picture)*

Left *A Dutch scene – cows, reeds and milk churns*

pen in Holland – you get rivers that run from mouth to source, rivers that are lower than the sea and rivers that turn into canals. We must follow the tortuous course of the Rhine through this strange landscape, although rivers may change their names and we may often lose our way.

In the last two thousand years the river has moved gradually towards the south, partly as a result of natural features like tides and partly as a result of the actions of man. Only about 250 years ago the delta used to begin in what is now Germany. Now it begins almost immediately you enter Holland, where the river divides into two main channels.

The landscape in this frontier area is quite different: a green, dim, rainy landscape, with woods, marshes, gravel-pits and canals. Once you get into Holland the ground becomes marshier, channels meander across the landscape with towpaths alongside them, cows graze in fields and sandhills can sometimes be seen in the distance. In some places this rather dull landscape is brightened in spring by fields of tulips, a Dutch speciality. As we get nearer the sea, onto the landscape that has been reclaimed from the sea, the fields become very straight, surrounded by canals, and windmills can be seen.

The German-Dutch frontier is reached at Emmerich in Holland, a small town with many sailors' pubs and cafés by the waterside from which one may listen to the hoots and toots of ships.

inland lake of the Netherlands: "A wise people provides for its future".

Land has been drained and dyked and great locks have been constructed on the rivers; a third of the Dutch land is below sea level. Due to this great activity by man, some strange things hap-

Right *Countryside in the Rhine delta*

In Holland the river divides into two channels, the greater and more southern of which is called the Waal. As we go on into Holland, this stream changes its name several times as it meets with other streams. Near Nijmegen it is just a short distance from the river Maas; only man's artificial works have kept the two rivers apart. The other main distributary becomes known as the Lek. What is officially still called the Rhine (Rijn in Dutch) eventually enters the sea, considerably

north of the main delta, as a small drainage canal – a strange end for such a mighty force of nature as the Rhine!

Near the river there is ill-drained and sometimes infertile land where few people live, although on the two main distributaries we would pass the twin cities of Nijmegen and Arnhem. These are forever associated with the tragic attempts at airborne landings by the Allies during the Second World War.

But we are not far from great cities, for, near the sea, is the great Dutch group of cities, the Randstad, or Ring City as it is known. It is called this because the towns stand in a ring round a central area that has been kept green and rural. It is only an hour's drive between the edge of this great city-group and the edge of the Ruhr. If they were to be joined together, an immense area of city would be created – along with even greater problems. Holland suffers greatly from pollution although the Dutch themselves are very careful – much of the polluted water is brought along the Rhine from France and Germany. The threat which this poses to life in the Dutch cities and to the wildlife of the remoter parts of the delta is very serious. The Dutch complain a great deal to those countries about this pollution.

At the end of our journey we come to the southern part of this group of cities. On the continuation of the Waal is the old town of Dordrecht. This used to be an attractive old Dutch town, with many beautiful brick houses with gables, and ringed round by canals. It was, however, terribly destroyed during the Second World War and only a little of the old centre is left – one of the saddest examples of the tragic destruction that Europe suffered.

Left *A bridge over the River Waal*

Above *This boat sailing over a road shows how inventive the Dutch have been in controlling water-flow*

On our journey we have passed through many great and busy cities, but as we approach the sea we come to one of the greatest of all – Rotterdam, just below where the old Maas and the Lek join. Since 1965, Rotterdam has been the busiest port in the whole world. This is the front door to the Rhine; it faces the North Sea and, beyond that, the ocean. On average a ship calls here every nineteen minutes! The pace of this great harbour and city never slackens, but the Rotterdam people also have pleasant uses for the water that brings them so much prosperity. They have one of the most famous yachting clubs in the world.

The harbour stands along the final waterway into which most of the waters of the Rhine flow. This is called the Nieuwe Maas. Near this area is the city centre which was destroyed by German bombers in 1940. Later, it was rebuilt mainly as a traffic-free centre – this has since become common, but Rotterdam was the first city to do it.

As we travel towards the open sea we see more and more docks along the Nieuwe Maas, for Rotterdam has coped with ever-larger ships, especially oil tankers and container ships. This section, which has been artificially widened, contains the great new "outport" of Europoort where many oil refineries can be seen beside the majestic waters. The latest Dutch effort has been to build new docks in the open sea itself! They are built in shallow water protected by a breakwater.

The end of the Nieuwe Maas is called the Hook of Holland, a bleak spot among sand-dunes where the warning light of the harbour marks one frontier of the river with the sea. It is here that we must take our leave of the Rhine, with the angry surf battering the land and with the lights of ships always to be seen in the distance. At its end the Rhine remains what it has always been – a great highway for man.

58 **Above** *Construction work on the Delta*

Above *Europoort – the great new port built for Rotterdam after the Second World War*

60 **Above** *Rotterdam – the busiest port in the world*

Glossary

Artery Important supply route, like the arteries that carry blood through the body.
Basin The area drained by a river and its *tributaries*.
Breakwater Barrier against the force of waves.
Canton A division of land, like a county or state. In Switzerland each canton has its own government.
Conurbation A large built-up area made up of various towns joined together.
Delta Triangular-shaped area at the mouth of a river.
Distributary A branch of a river running into the sea, usually at its *delta*.
Dyke A bank of earth and stones built to prevent low-lying land being flooded.
Fault Lines of weakness in the earth's crust, causing rocks to sink.
Fertile land Fruitful, rich land good for growing crops on.
Geology Study of the make-up of the earth.
Glacier Mass of ice which moves slowly down a valley from high mountains.
Gorge Deep, narrow valley with steep walls.
Headstream Stream which is a source of a river.
Industrial Revolution Period during the eighteenth and nineteenth centuries when the invention of machinery led to the setting up of factories and large-scale industry.

Lock Walled-in section of a canal or river where water levels can be changed for raising and lowering boats.
Meanders Large curves and loops in the course of a river.
Megalopolis An enormous built-up area.
Middle Ages The period between the fifth and fifteenth centuries.
Pilot A guide: a river pilot guides ships through difficult stretches of water.
Pollution Land, water or air made unclean and unhealthy.
Principality Land ruled by a prince.
Reformation Great religious revolution of the sixteenth century when Protestant churches broke away from Roman Catholicism.
Rift valley Valley formed when land between two *faults* sinks down.
Rural Of the countryside.
Sediment Material, carried in riverwater which sinks to the river bed.
Tributary River or stream running into another, usually larger, one.
Volcanic Formed by a volcano.

Facts and Figures

Length of Rhine: 1,320 km (820 miles).
Area of Rhine drainage basin: 223,000 sq km (86,000 sq miles).
Width at Köln: 460 m (1,500 ft).
Total Rhine trade (for 1965): 228 million tonnes (225 million tons).

Time Chart

c. 100 BC–AD 300   The Roman Empire gains and holds control over the Rhineland area; extensive Rhine trade first develops.
c. AD 500–1500   Medieval period; various rulers hold control over Rhineland area; at first there is political disorder, but then peasant farming and trade develop.
c. 1500–1650   Period of the Protestant Reformation.
c. 1750–1900   Period of the Industrial Revolution; industry develops and problems of pollution begin.
1816   First steamship on the Rhine.
1871   Unification of Germany; commercial development speeds up and an era of canal building and improvement of navigation gets fully under way.
1901   River fully navigable as far inland as Basel.
1939–45   Period of the Second World War, after which Germany is split into two. Many of the last battles of the war fought near the Rhine and Rhine cities heavily bombed.
1989   Date by which it is planned the Rhine–Danube canal system will be in full operation, forming a great international waterway.

Further Reading

Finley, D., *The Rhine* (Macdonald Educational, 1975)

Mackinder, H. J., *The Rhine* (Chatto and Windus, 1908)

Marsden, W., *The Rhineland* (Batsford, 1973)

Pilkington, R., *Small Boat on the Lower Rhine* (Macmillan, 1970)

Pilkington, R., *Small Boat on the Upper Rhine* (Macmillan, 1971)

Whittam, E., *The Rhine* (Oxford University Press, 1962)

ACKNOWLEDGEMENTS

Aerofilms Limited, 24; Camera Press, *frontispiece*, 31, 32, 46, 47, 48, 50; J. Allen Cash, 43; Douglas Dickins, 21; Fremdenverkehrsverband Rheinland-Pfalz, 36 (Bohm), 39 (Ganzhubner); Eric Hosking, 12; NASA, 52; Netherlands National Tourist Board, 54, 55, 56, 57,58; Picturepoint – London, 34, 37, 38, 40, 44, 49, 51; Radio Times, 28 *(left)*, 30; Ronald Sheridan, 11 *(top right)*, 14, 16, 29, 41; Spectrum Colour Library, 28 *(right)*, 42, 58, 59, 60–1; Swiss National Tourist Office, 8, 9, 13, 17, 18, 19, 20, 22–3, 27; Wayland Picture Library, 33. Artwork by Alan Gunston, Michael Paysden and Celia Ware.

Index

Adenauer, Konrad 46
Alps 9, 10, 12, 15, 16, 18, 25
Arnhem 57
Austria 9, 19, 20

Baden-Baden 31
Basel 23, 25, 26, 29
Bingen 25, 35, 39
Black Forest mountains 26, 28
Bonn 35, 43, 46, 47

Castles 35, 36
Celts 10, 31
Chur 18
Climate 16, 28
Constance, Lake of 23
Conurbations 32, 45, 49, 50, 5

Danube River 9
Dordrecht 57
Drachenfels 43
Duisburg 50
Düsseldorf 45, 49

Emmerich 54
Europoort 58

Farming 16, 28, 29, 38, 54
France 9, 23, 25, 28, 29, 31, 53
Frankfurt 32
Freiburg 31

Germany and Germany, West 9, 10, 23, 25, 28, 29, 31, 32, 35, 36, 38, 39, 40, 43, 45, 46, 47, 49, 50, 54
Grisons, Canton of 16

Hatto of Mainz 36
Heine, Heinrich 39, 40
Hitler, Adolf 40, 43
Hook of Holland 58

Industry 26, 31, 32, 45, 49, 50, 58

Juf 16

Karlsruhe 31
Koblenz 35, 39, 40
Köln 49

Lahn River 40
Lek distributary 56
Liechtenstein 9, 19, 20
Lorelei rock and song 39, 40
Luther, Martin 32

Maas River 53, 56, 58
Mainz 32
Mannheim 32
Megalopolis 10, 32, 57
Moselle River 40
Mouse Tower 36

Nazis 40, 43, 46
Neanderthal Man 9, 49, 50
Neckar River 32
Netherlands 9, 53, 54, 56, 57, 58
Nibelungs, legends of 43
Nieuwe Maas 58
Nijmegen 56, 57

Pfalz of Kaub 36
Pilots 38
Pollution 10, 26, 45, 47, 48, 57

Randstad 57
Reformation 32
Reichenau 19
Remagen, bridge at 40, 43
Rheingar 32
Rheinwaldhorn Glacier 15
Rhine
  canals 9, 29, 50, 54, 57
  delta 53, 54, 56, 57, 58
  drainage basin 9
  dyking and draining 54, 57
  floods, control of 20, 23, 53
  formation of 10, 12
  gorge 35, 36, 38, 39, 40, 43
  Hinter Rhine 15, 16, 18
  length 9
  meanders 29
  navigation, control of 38, 39, 50, 58
  sedimentation 12, 53
  shifts in course 29, 54
  sources 9, 15, 19
  traffic on 9, 23, 26, 29, 36, 38, 47, 50, 58
  Vorder Rhine 19
Rhône River 9
Rift valley 25
Romans, ancient 9, 18, 32, 40, 49
Romansch 16
Rotterdam 58
Ruhr region 45, 50, 57

Schaffhausen, falls at 23
Schams, valley of 16
Scheldt River 53
Second World War 10, 40, 43, 49, 57, 58
Siebengebirge 43
Snow White 43
Speyer 32
Strasbourg 29, 31
Switzerland 9, 15, 16, 18, 19, 20, 23, 25, 26

Taunus mountains 32
Terraces, river 29

Vegetation 16, 28, 54
Veranhof 23
Via Mala 16, 18
Vosges mountains 28

Waal distributary 56, 57
Wagner, Richard 43
Wildlife 26, 31, 47, 57
Wine growing 28, 32, 36, 38, 40
Worms and Worms, Diet of 32

Zuider Zee 53, 54